Before the Victorian era, the ordinary people of this c
outdoor lives, despite the uncertain climate. The home was
the weary head at night, but it was in the streets and public pl.... .....- ....st of life
was spent.

In Newcastle and Gateshead, this generally meant on the "Kee", where all of life's joys and hazards could be encountered, and all transactions were carried out under smoky grey skies. For on those ancient cobbles you could witness almost every kind of human activity, meet a rich variety of "characters" and, if it was to your taste, be guaranteed free entertainment for every day of your life. From the Sandhill, that ancient triangular *piazza* which had once been a public beach, to the Sandgate, stretched Newcastle "Kee", with its warren of steep chares leading off. And over the Old Tyne Bridge in Gateshead were Hillgate and Pipewellgate, with their narrow cobbled streets, towering tenements and warehouses with river frontage, all equally packed with life. This was the province of the working people of Tyneside. Here roamed the sturdy, unruly mob who gave the area its distinctive characteristic, the "Folk doon on the Kee".

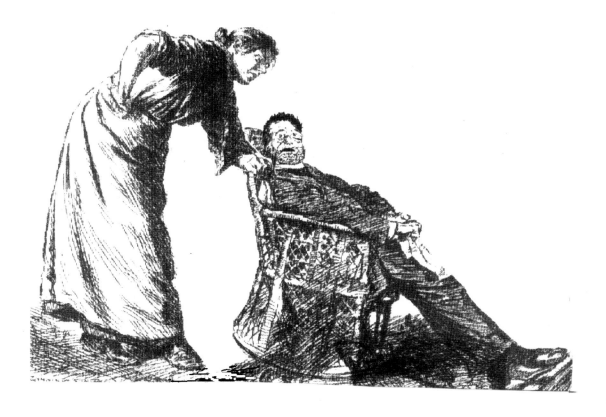

"Now then, laddie, ye're next!"

Market days were perhaps the best time to observe quayside life, for on those days the "Kee" was graced with the "shavers", a flock of ragmuffin women who would, for half the cost of a regular barber, "shave ye t'the bone". Many were the idlers who stood about guffawing and enjoying the spectacle as the victims writhed under the "chop-torturing tools" of the merciless harridans. Presumably there was an endless supply of unsuspecting out-of-towners, sailors, pitmen and the like.

As can be seen from Willy Stephenson's poem, an extract of which follows, the experience of the shearing was not one to be undergone lightly!

The Quayside Shaver

On each markit day, sor, the folks of the Kee, sor,
Gan flockin' wi' beards they hev sivvin days worn,
And roond the Sandgate, sor, in crowds they aal wait, sor,
T'git thasells shaved in rotatitive torn.
Owld sowljas on sticks, sor, about poly-ticks, sor,
Debate, til at length quite heated they've grown,
But none may escape, sor, til owld Madam Scrape, sor,
Cries oot "whie's next, lads, t'sit thasells doon?"

There's pitmen wi' baskits and fine posy weskits,
That talks aboot nowt but whie hews and puts best,
Then Keelmen jist landed swears "may they be stranded,
If they're not shaved FORST, by the quickest and best!"
Wi' their face full of coal-dust, they'd frighten ye almost,
As they fling off their hats while usorpin' the chair,
While others stand fumin' and think it provokin',
There's nee-one sez owt, cos there's nee-one wad dare!

No sooner the razor's laid on t' the face, sor,
Than painful distortions tek place on the brow,
But if they complain, sor, they'll find it in vain, sor,
Though yellin' an' swearin' and loud shouts of "HOW!"
And as she scrapes roond them, if she chance t' wound them,
They'll cry out as though she'd deprived them of life,
"Odd smash ya brains, wummin, ah feel the blood cummin',
Ah'd rather be shaved wi' an owld gully knife!"

For all they can say, sor, she still rasps away, sor,
An' sweeps roond their jaw the chop-torturin' tool,
Til they in a fret, sor, do beg her to whet, sor,
But she gives the answer "be still, ye geet fyeul!"
For all their repinin', their twistin' an' whinin',
She forward cracks on til she's mown off the hair
And, finished, cries "there, sor!", they leap from the chair, sor,
Cryin' "Smash man, ye bugga, ye've scraped me bones bare!"

The pitmen mentioned in the poem certainly brought their own "characters" with them on days when they visited "toon". One of the most famous among them was Tom Dixon of Low Fell, who was celebrated as the greatest "booler" of his age. The kind of "booling" he excelled in was not "crown green", however, and it *certainly* wasn't cricket!

The pitmen of that time indulged themselves in a much wilder form of the sport known as *lane* booling in which the "bool" was hurled as far as possible down a public highway with the speed and trajectory of a cannonball. Woe betide any unfortunate travellers who happened to be in the road when the "bools" were cast! Many was the broken limb which resulted and many was the broken head which was wreaked in revenge! Of course, the principal interest in the result of a "booling" contest was due to the bets which had been placed on the outcome, and sometimes many pounds changed hands after a match. There were many fanatical gamblers among the pitmen, as evidenced in this extract from Thomas Wilson's poem "Pitman's Pay";

Watch Yasells!
Tom Dixon prepares to cast

"See on the right a gambling few
  Whose every word and look display
  A desperate, dark, designing crew,
  Intent upon each other's pay."

They're racers, cockers, carders keen,
  As ever o'er a tankard met,
  Or ever booled a match between
  The Poplin Well and Mawvin's Yett."

Here, Tom, the pick of boolers gained,
  Himself a never-dying fame,
  By deeds wherein an ardour reigned,
  Which neither age nor toil could tame."

Despite his success and the number of "backers" he enjoyed, however, Tom Dixon saw very little of the winnings, and died a poor man at the *Black Ram* tavern, Low Fell, in 1828. He was eighty-five years of age and was so famous that his decease was mentioned in the local paper. He'd gone on "booling" until the very end, sometimes casting down the Fell lanes alone, if he couldn't find a match.

Benwell Staithes, showing a chauldron of coal going down to the keels

Of course pitmen didn't gamble away *all* their earnings. They sometimes spent their money on more sensible things like getting drunk. At times like this, they would descend upon the quayside taverns and get up a "rant", such as is described in Henry Robson's *Collier's Pay Week*, an edited version of which follows. This sort of breezy song gives the lie to the common misconception that the industrial revolution brought nothing but misery to the working classes.

Ordinary people, especially Tynesiders, will always find a way to enjoy themselves and the pitmen were certainly not in the least backward at "pushing the boat out"! Unfortunately, the "boat" sometimes carried them into deep waters, as can be seen in this song as it wends to its riotous conclusion.

Thomas Wilson, Pitman Poet

"The baff week is o'er, no repining,
  Pay-Saturday's swift on the wing,
  At length the blythe morning comes shining
  When kelter makes colliers sing!

Bob Cranky, Jack Hogg and Bob Marley,
Bill Hewitt, Luke Carr and Tom Broon,
In one jolly squad set off early,
From Benwell t' Newcassel toon.

And now the next house they've agreed on
Not far from the head of the Kee
Where they wi' black puddins might feed on
And spend the remains of the day.

Bob vowed he wad hev some fine caperin',
Jist as soon as his dinner was o'er,
Wi' the lassie that wore the white apron,
Who was reelin' about on the floor."

"Their meal being done then rose Bob up,
He wished to indulge in a jig,
But a Willington lad set his gob up,
And swore he wad give him a dig!

When sober, a mild man was Marley,
More apt to join friends than make foes,
But raised by the juice of the barley,
He put in some canny shrewd blows!

All hand-o'er-heed, topsy-turvy,
They struck wi' fists, elbows and feet,
A Willington lad they called Gurvey,
Went tops-o'er-tails off his seat.

Luke Carr had one eye closed entire,
And what was a turrible farce,
Poor Robin was cast on the fire,
And tasted the coals wi' his arse!

How the wayfaring companies parted,
The muse chooses not to proclaim,
But battered and bruised and down-hearted,
At last they went toddling hame.

Now ye Collier Callants so clever,
Residing 'twixt Tyne and the Wear,
Beware when ye fuddle together,
Of makin' too free wi' strang beer!"

The lads of Benwell Pit were well known for their excesses and were sometimes even foolish enough to tangle with the Keelmen when filled to overflowing with "Dutch courage". I imagine many a Benwell lad ended his "day oot on the Kee" by sitting up to his neck in the "Coaly Old Tyne"!

The "Coaly Old Tyne"

Besides the "Shavers", there were many other persons plying their trade in the open air "doon on the kee". One of the more colourful of these was the husband and wife team, Bella and Tommy Laing, who were often referred to as "Alpha and Omega" (A and Z) because of their respective professions. Bella was a "howdy", which is to say a local midwife, and could also be relied upon to provide other more discreet services for local lassies who were not so delighted with their condition. Her husband, Tommy, was a coffin-maker and kept a hearse, so their partnership thrived no matter how the birth turned out!

It's anither one for ye, Tommy, ah's afeared

Bella joined the mourners at all of the funerals too, at which time she was able to meet prospective customers and advertise her trade among the ladies. The enterprising couple were so successful that they became quite rich, investing their earnings in property and even having houses built to order. The square which went by the name of "Laing's Corner" was built by them and willed to their children when they died.

Cuckoo Jack

Another "character" who thrived on other's misfortune was "Cuckoo Jack" (John Wilson) who became so expert at dredging dead bodies out of the Tyne that he was regularly employed by the Corporation to perform this service. He was paid at the rate of from ten to fifteen shillings a corpse (depending on size and gender!) and it was said that he would refuse to rescue a drowning person on the grounds that he could get more for the corpse!

He lived on Sandgate Shore and could often be seen poling about off the Kee sounding for business. He was a waterman by training but made so much money at the dredging (he also sold back items like watches, jewelry etc which had fallen in the river) that he gave up his trade to concentrate on his art. No man knew the river better than Jack and even the keelmen knew less about the depths, shoals and currents which lay between the "Kees". Using his knowledge of the river bed and its currents, he designed his own dredging tackle which was efficient in all circumstances at grappling and raising items from the river bed. Finally, he became so well-respected for his rivercraft that, late in life, he was appointed Assistant to the Quay Master.

One of his more comical characteristics was his practice of having breakfast before he went to bed. Apparently, he had to rise so early in the morning to "ketch the neet's corpses" that he had no time to take breakfast and he had such a huge appetite that he was loathe to miss a meal!

Jack died on December the 2nd, 1860, aged 68, and was noteworthy enough to have a humorous lament written on his death. The famous Ned Corvan (he who wrote *The Fishermen Hung the Monkey-O!*) wrote the song and performed it regularly at his Music Hall in Wapping Street, South Shields. An extract follows;

> "Wye luika here, doon belaw,
> Ah've hook'd him now, less his jaw!
> And thet meks a hundred an' sivvinty-nine
> Deed bodies ah've fished from the rivva Tyne!"

Ned Corvan's songs tended to be medleys of tunes interspersed with comic dialogue and another part of the "lament", sung to the tune of *The Keel Row* was;

> "Fareweel to me cronies,
> Keeside and Sandgit Joanies,
> For achin' ev'ry bone is,
> In this owld skin o'mine.

Despite the comic aspects of Jack's work and behaviour, he well known as one of the most unsmiling characters you could ever expect to meet. As Ned Corvan said of him; "His fyess didn't knaa HOW to laff…."

The true genius of Ned Corvan was that he often wrote his songs overnight, to respond to the latest news, so that his material would be topical. He was one of the greatest writers and performers of the early Music Hall and had been a "character" himself on the "Kee", having been brought up in Newcastle before moving to South Shields. When his health was broken by drink and his voice reduced to a hoarse whisper, Ned moved back to Newcastle and could often be seen sitting around the pubs and taverns soliciting drinks on the strength of his reputation. He died on the 31st August, 1865, and was buried in St Andrew's churchyard. Newcastle, without a headstone. He was only 35 years old.

Ned Corvan
(wanted dead or alive in Hartlepool)

Another famous "Keeside witch" was simply known as "Owld Mabel". Although Thomas Wilson, the pitman poet, who knew her well, declared her to be harmless and not able to do more than "raise a wind to shake a neighbour's roof", he did concede that she had a remarkable memory.

Apparently she could recall the exact date and even time of the births and deaths of all who lived within five miles of her home and could tell who "came again", in what form, and what must be done to lay them finally to rest. In this last respect, she offered her services to local preachers, priests and the like, though whether they took her up on her offer was a different matter. She also knew all the haunted houses in the area, who haunted them, and why! As Wilson remarked, she "made much business with credulous folk" and was a "terror to the rough, rollicking pitmen".

Owld Mabel

Of course, not all Tyneside women of that era were fierce harridans. Although more celebrated for their utility than their beauty, there *were* some fine-looking lassies amongst the womenfolk "doon on the Kee". Judging from the street-ballads, there were even some rough beauties among the "yella girls", before hard work stole away the bloom of their youth.

Such a beauty was Sally Wheatley, who inspired the very wistful and haunting little song, written by the great Joe Wilson, which follows. If Sally did eventually marry her Mr Black, she will have done very well for herself, for I suspect him to have been Mr Charles Alexander Black, who was a check-weighman on the "Kee", a position of great power and responsibility.

In any event, poor Joe Wilson stood little chance. Music Hall performers, even if they were immensely popular, earned little more than "beer money" in those days and, despite the great songs he wrote, Joe Wilson was no exception. He ran a boarding house to supplement his meagre income.

Sally Wheatley

Now ah'm most put oot and sad, when ah once was blithe and glad
Ah used t' trip aroond the toon sae lithe and neatly
Ah was happy night an' morn, now of all such joys ah'm shorn
Since ah fell sae deep in love wi' Sally Wheatley.

Chorus;
And it's oh dear me, what am ah gan t'dee
Sally's gone an' tuk away me heart completely,
And ah'll nivvor get it back, 'cos she gans wi' Mr Black,
And they say he's gan t'marry Sally Wheatley.

Wye ah've nivvor seen such a lass, though ah knaa she likes her glass
She could toss a pot of ale back nice and sweetly,
Wye it's reet t' tek a drop, if y' knaa jist when t' stop,
That was jist the very way wi' Sally Wheatley.

How ah felt ah divvint knaa, when that lass forst time ah saw,
In a threesome reel sh' hopped aboot right leetly,
And ah might hev had a chance if ah'd asked her up t' dance,
But ah was ower shy t' speak t' Sally Wheatley.

So as often is the case, ye'll find others in your place,
If ye divvint shove ahead an' fettle reetly,
For ah'd scarcely torned me back, aye an' there was Mr Black,
An' he was jiggin' roond the room wi' Sally Wheatley.

Well he must hev made it right when he set her yem that night,
Cos, aal dressed up, he gans t' see her neetly,
Wye there's danger in delay, or ah'd not be sad today,
And ah've lost me poor owld heart t' Sally Wheatley.

Sally walks out with Mr Black

But another of Joe Wilson's songs, which follows overleaf, is more typical of the rough courting practices of the "folk doon on the Kee".

Me Bonny Gatesheed Lass

"Ah warrant ye'll not knaa me lass,
Hor name ah dorsint mention, man,
For fear ye'll gang an tell her
How ah love hor, so ah dee,
Cos it's jist for lads and lasses, now,
T'whispa their affections and
The bonniest lass in Gatesheed's bonny face has bothered me!

Well, the forst time that ah saw that lass,
Ah thought ah didn't knaa hor but
Ah was sure ah'd seen hor face before
And ah didn't knaa from where.
Hor blue eyes met mine in passing on
The High Street in the mornin and
Hor look was so entrancin' that me heart was mine nee mair!

Wye ah didn't see hor for a week
Til one neet at the bridge end when
Ah trampled on hor goon and
The gathers came away!
She sez ah was ah clumsy lout
An glowered at me hobnail boots
Man, ah humbly begged hor pardon, ah was licked for what t'say!

Wye ah walked alang beside hor
Jist as if ah had a right t'dee.
The conversation forst was shy,
But then it torned forst class,
We talked aboot the weather then
She mentioned that hor father was
A puddler doon at Hawkses, oh me bonny Gatesheed lass!

She mentioned, confidentially, that
Hor uncle was a grocer and
Hor mother's father's cousin was
A fiddler on the shore.
She talked so nice and friendly and
She looked so sweet and pleasant that
Ah thowt ah'd nivvor seen a lass sae charmin' like before!

Ah mek hor laff an' slap me lug
Wi' talkin' lots o' nonsense but,
Bless ye, when ye're courting, man
There's nowt sae gud'll pass.
Ah axed hor wad she be me lass,
Step oot wi' me on Sundays and
To my delight, she sez "ah might", me bonny Gatesheed lass!

The Tyne was in a dreadful state in those days, silted and shoaled and very hazardous to navigate. But no matter how neglected the state of the river, Newcastle was always one of the major ports of the realm so that many of the "folk doon on the Kee" were visiting sailors, men of all nationalities and persuasions, and those who served and preyed upon them. There were, of course, many "characters" among those who helped them to spend their hard-earned shillings

"Sailors Carousing", from a painting by Sutherland

Besides the "Yella Girls", who could always be persuaded to join in any intemperate behaviour which was going on, there were others who were more than willing to help matters along. Among the most notable of the "ladies of the Kee" were Squinting Meg and Oyster Mally, who offered more than mere seafood to the young tars when they were on a spree. The short ditty overleaf, by Henry Robson, immortalises these two "beauties" and gives the flavour of a typical "run ashore"; with all its joys and hazards;

Til the Tide Cums In

"While strolling doon sweet Sangit Street
An owld shipmate ah chanc'd to meet
To the sign of *The Ship* ah hauled him in
T' drink a gud glass, til the tide cums in.

Ah tuk in tow young Squinting Meg
Whie knaas very fine how t' shake hor leg
Me mate hauled Oyster Mally in
And we jigged them aboot til the tide came in

We boosed away til break of day
Then asked "what shot we'd hev t' pay"
"Ye've drank" said the Host "nine pints of gin"
So we paid him his due, cos the tide was in.

Shipping at Glass House Bridge, near Byker

18

But other, more serious, dangers lay in wait for unsuspecting sailors who were out for a good time on the Kee, for His Majesty's Press maintained a permanent presence in the port.

The depradations of His Majesty's officers did not pass without resistance, however, and there were many pitched battles fought on the Kee between the Press Gang and their intended victims. It was, indeed, a hard fate for a poor sailor, returning home after a long voyage of perhaps as much as two years, to be caught by the Press Gang and hustled off to sea before he could even see his wife and children again.

> "The Press hev took wor Willie
> While he was all alone,
> He bravely fought for liberty
> But there was three to one.
> The blood it flowed in torrents,
> He cried "Oh pray, kill me!
> I'd rather die for Mary's sake
> Than gang back on the sea".

The Keelmen, in particular, resented any of their number being forced into the Service and many a broken head was dealt out when the Press were audacious enough to attempt to "steal" a Keelman they had caught alone or unawares. The battles grew so severe that "local annals teem with records of riot and violence", to quote Salmon, the South Shields historian. Indeed, many times the tables were turned and the Press Gang themselves dared not venture out on the Quay for fear of the vengeful citizens who lay in wait for them. On some occasions, marines had to be landed from His Majesty's ships to rescue the beleaguered Pressmen. Eventually, the Press were reduced to cruising off the river mouth in their tender (boat), making occasional forays when they thought the "defenders" on the shore were unawares;

> "Here's the tender cummin'
> Pressin' all the men.
> Oh dearie hinny
> What shall we do then?
> Here's the tender cummin'
> Off at Sheels bar
> Here's the tender cummin'
> Full of men o' war!
>
> Hey bonnie laddie
> Let's gan tee the Lawe
> And see the tender lying
> Off at Sheels bar,
> With hor colours a-flyin'
> And hor anchor at hor bow,
> They've tuk me bonnie laddie
> What shall ah dee now?"

His Majesty's Press at Work

Some sort of order was finally restored by Captain John Bouvier, who was appointed to command the Press and act as Regulating Officer to the Port of Tyne during the American War of Independence. This brave and gallant officer, known locally as "Captain Bovver" (pronounced like "bother") showed a remarkable good sense in striking a balance between the necessity to man His Majesty's ships and the needs and prejudices of the local community. He set up Press Appeal Courts, whereby a pressed man could appeal against impressments or at least gain the right to settle his affairs before being rushed off to sea. He also issued exemption certificates to the Keelmen, declaring their industry to be "essential to the peace of the Realm", although some thought that their exemption was more likely to be "essential to the peace of the Press Gang"!

To a certain degree, despite his occupation, Captain "Bovver" even became quite popular locally, or at very least respected, so that his funeral on May the 20th, 1782, was attended by thousands. The combined bands of the local militia regiments, plus the Cameronians from the barracks, marched behind the coffin and the dead march was played as the procession wound its way up from the Quayside to the Bigg Market, where Bover had lodged. Full Civic honours were accorded to the deceased, the Mayor and all civic dignitaries turning out. Most importantly, the mob behaved respectfully, no-one stoned the coffin and, amazingly for *any* public occasion, there was not even a single arrest..

Grenadiers fired three volleys over the grave as he was laid to rest in St Nicholas' Churchyard. He had been Regulating Officer in the port for over 24 years and all agreed that he had carried out his duties fairly and with restraint.

His good reputation didn't save him from *some* notoriety in the ballads of the "Kee", however, as may be deduced from the following fragment. The original version of this song may be traced back to Queen Anne's time, at the turn of the eighteenth century, but it was adapted to incorporate the good Captain's name later in the century. This was fame indeed!

"Where hev ye been, my canny hinny?
Where hev ye been, my winsome
                               young man?
Ah've been to the Nor'ard
Cruised backward an' for'ard,
But Ah daresint step ashore now
For Bovver's foul gang!"

Captain Bovver ponders a difficult case at the Press Appeals Court

Like Hyde Park Corner, the "Kee" had its fair share of "ravers", as they were locally known. Possibly the most colourful of these was Billy Scott, universally known as "Cull Billy", who was capable of declaiming faultlessly from scripture in such a clear and exact manner that he often gathered a crowd, albeit of scoffers and idlers, who usually crowned his efforts with a shower of dirt and stones.

Though considered "cull" (a simpleton), Billy often surprised the unwary with the sharpness of his wit. Once, for instance, when a pompous citizen found Billy blocking his way and peremptorily barked "out of my way, I never give place to fools!" Billy replied "I do" and stepped aside.

The following verses by Robert Emery
give another example of Cull Billy's wit;

"As Billy Scott was on the trot alang the
Puddin' Chare,
A shillin' on the pavement lay which Billy
soon with care
Into his breeches pocket put and trotted on
with glee
But a wag, who'd seen him stoop, cried out
"Hey! That belangs t'me!"

Poor Billy gravely turned about and thus
did him accost;
"Can you, upon your honour, say, a sixpence
you have lost?"
"I have indeed!" the wag replied. Says Bill
"I must away,
Cos it's a shillin' I have found. I thank ye,
sir, good day!"

Cull Billy, "Raving"

Another famous "raver" of the quayside was none other than the older brother of the famous artist, John Martin, R.A.

William Martin, or "the philosophical conqueror of all nations" as he styled himself, was a frequent soap-box orator on the "Kee". He declared himself to have been "chosen by God to reveal the mysteries of the universe" and particularly objected to the scientific theories of Sir Isaac Newton, whom he declared to be nothing more or less than a "knave and a deceiver of Mankind".

Despite his eccentricities, however, "Billy" Martin was an accomplished poet, artist and engraver, producing his own self-publicising handbills, one of which is reproduced below;

Eventually, whether motivated by brotherly love or just plain embarrassment, his famous younger brother invited him to London to live with him and Tyneside lost forever one of the best-known "characters" of the "Kee". The great "philosopher" languished in his new surroundings, however, and died two years later, in 1851.

All good things come to an end, and the best of things go with a bang and not with a whimper. Such was the case, quite literally, with the "Kee". A terrific explosion on the night of the 6th October, 1854, which started with a fire on the Gateshead side, levelled so many buildings on each quayside that the Corporation had the excuse to carry out a "major redevelopment" of the area. All the old wynds and chares were levelled and all the old "characters" who used to infest them were turfed out. Gone forever were the "Folk doon on the Kee" and with them the vibrant lifestyle which had enhanced Tyneside life. As Johnson says in his excellent book *The Making of the River Tyne*;

"In place of the line of small tradesmen's shops and inns....there are now tall stone blocks of offices, where the business of collieries and cargo steamers are transacted. The tradesmen have migrated "up-street" and have left the Quayside to the habitues of the Exchange, who morning and afternoon are to be seen "on the front", seeking or settling charters and buying and selling coals."

The town may have gained economically, but in social terms, the rich traders were a poor substitute for Blind Willie and his friends. One hopes that, at very least, Jeannie Jamieson's ghost stayed behind to haunt them as they counted their money! In the words of an anonymous poet;

"Farewell to the bruisers, the bully-boys and boosers,
Farewell to Cull Billy and owld Blind Willie tee!
Nee mair we'll see the shavers, the yella girls and ravers,
Cos Charlie Bertram's pooder-house has blawn them off the Kee"

The Old Kee during the inundation of the Great Flood of 1771

The Fire Doon on the Kee

(Tyneside's Biggest Disaster)

The remains of Bertram's Warehouse just before the blast

Just after three o'clock in the morning of Friday October the 6th, 1854, a little girl came crying to her mother's bed in South Shields. She had been disturbed from her slumbers by the sound and vibration of a tremendous explosion, so violent that it filled her with terror and drove her to seek the comfort of her mother's arms. She was not to know that the explosion which had awakened her had occurred on Gateshead Quay, some eight miles away.

Meanwhile, across the river, in North Shields, a gentleman who had risen early to travel on business found that his hair brushes were shaken off his dressing table by the vibration, which he likened to an earthquake in its force.

When these events occurred, the fire which had caused them had already been raging for over two hours. It was a conflagration which was to engulf not only the riverside at Gateshead, but also the greater part of Newcastle Quay, a fire which was to alter the appearance of those ancient centres of commerce forever.

Prior to the Great Fire (or "The Fire Doon on the Kee", as it became colloquially known) the riverside had been a virtual warren of narrow, congested wynds and chares, with its tall tenement buildings packed with humanity, living in dreadfully insanitary conditions, cheek by jowl. The ancient timber-framed buildings leaned crazily one against the other, some almost touching one another on opposite sides of the street, many of them heavily shored and propped as they tended to slippage down the steep riverbank towards the quay. The impression given was that, if one fell, they would all fall down.

Many of the narrow chares on the Newcastle side had not altered substantially since medieval times. Indeed, the only major alteration in the appearance of Newcastle's riverside had occurred in the middle of the previous century, when one end of the nave of the medieval church which served the area, All Hallows, had collapsed, slipping down the steep bank into the river, so that the church had had to be demolished and a new one built.

Serious cholera epidemics, the last of which had occurred in 1853, had led the leading citizens of the town to call for a general demolition and redevelopment of the area, but such proposals were met with great suspicion and stout resistance from those who dwelled there. Although over1500 of them had perished in five weeks during that last dreadful outbreak, the poorer citizens stood firm against change. Quite rightly as it turned out, they suspected that, once rooted out, they would never get back.

People preferred the "devil they knew" to the fine promises of the politicians and gentry of the town. Relations between the poorer citizens and the Corporation, dominated as it was by "hostmen" (coal-owners), had always been strained and had even caused working men to locate their institutions beyond the town limits to avoid the Corporation's corrupt control. The Keelmen, for instance, who had raised a levy on their members to build their own church and hospital, had been careful to build them outside the Sandgate, in an effort to keep them from the clutches of the Corporation.

Medieval street with jettied housing, similar to Newcastle's chares

Among the first to witness the beginnings of the Great Fire were two railwaymen, who had been out all night working a pilot engine between Gateshead and Newcastle. In those days of high consumption rates and limited coal and water-carrying capacity, pilot engines were often provided at stations to bring the train safely in whilst mainline engines were refuelled or relieved. From their vantage point as they crossed back and forth on the High Level Bridge, they saw "the first *spirits* of fire at Gateshead and had observed how the blue flame crept from window to window in the darkness" as the fire progressed through the warehouses on Gateshead Quay.

In fact, later investigations revealed that the fire had broken out at about half past midnight in Wilson's worsted manufactory, where large quantities of combustible materials were stored. Wool, and the oil and soap used in its preparation, were present in abundance and the premises itself was lit by gas. Furthermore, there was a boiler room in the basement, used for drying purposes, and this was not ceiled, so that it was possible for waste from the manufactory to fall through the floorboards and down into the boiler room below. Messrs Wilson, however, later claimed that the boiler furnace was thoroughly damped each night, the waste removed regularly, and the gas turned off at the mains.

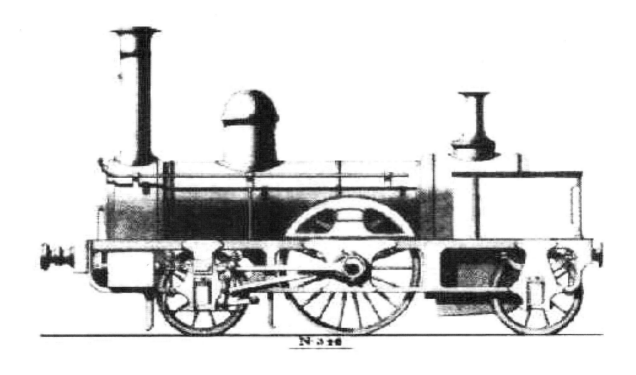

Type of locomotive used for " piloting" in the 1850s

Whatever had been the cause of the fire, there was no doubt that it had originated in Wilson's premises. A Newcastle policeman, John Ewart, had been the first to spot spot the glow from the Newcastle side and had hastened across the river after alerting the authorites. The fire being on the low side of the building, it was not immediately visible in Gateshead. Meeting with Walter Scott, a Gateshead policeman, in Hillgate, the two had entered the blazing premises to find the fire "burning fiercely, as if it had been burning for some time". They awoke the "watchman", the owner's nephew John Wilson, who was blissfully unaware that anything was amiss.

Old bonded warehouses at Newcastle of a similar type to Bertram's
These, too, fell victims to fire, being burned by vandals in recent years

At about two o'clock, when the fire engines and the volunteers who manned them arrived, they could only turn their attention to the neighbouring premises, Wilson's manufactory being totally engulfed.

And now the windows of the substantial building next door, Bertram's bonded warehouse, burst inwards with a crack, admitting the flames. This huge premises, fully eighty feet long and seven stories in height, contained much combustible material, including hundreds of tons of sulphur.

An officer of the 26th Regiment in the 1850s

Drawn from their beds by the excitement, large crowds had begun to gather on Newcastle Quay to witness the spectacle. Wilson's factory was ablaze from top to bottom and, despite the efforts of the firemen, the fire was taking a hold in the vast warehouse next door. Flames of every colour and intensity now began to leap from window to window as the conflagration spread from floor to floor. There were gasps of surprise and delight from the crowds, which grew by the minute, as though they were watching a firework display or other such staged spectacle. The Old Tyne Bridge itself was so packed that there was no thoroughfare to cross.

By the time that the soldiers of the garrison arrived on the scene to re-inforce the firefighters at about three o'clock, every floor of the warehouse was ablaze, the contents burning with all the colours of the rainbow.

Ensign Paynter, with a sergeant and fifty soldiers of the 26th regiment, the Cameronians, immediately began to set up their engines to help the local volunteer brigade contain the blaze. Being required to tackle the blaze at the rear of the building, Ensign Paynter went with his men to supervise the fitting of the suction pipe into the river.

It was then that the explosion occurred.

Ensign Paynter, two of his soldiers and three firemen were killed on the spot and, as the *North & South Shields Gazette* reported "it is painful to speculate on the number of persons that must have perished among the ruins". For not only were Wilson's Manufactory and Bertram's Warehouse destroyed in the enormous blast, but also the whole of that end of Hillgate, including many ramshackle lodgings in which working class families were packed, many to a stair-head.

Everywhere, above the roar and crackle of the flames, the "sound of wailing could be heard. Men were in tears." In one place a woman begged passers-by to help her rescue her child, on whom the roof had fallen whilst it lay in bed, but to no avail, all was confusion. The sulphurous fumes released from the warehouse fatally hampered rescue efforts and proved destructive to the dying.

The Church of St Mary, on its hill above the quayside, "was a wreck, its windows broken and the roof destroyed". Its illuminated clock was in ruins, though the immobile pointers told the time of the explosion for all to see, ten past three. Massive chunks of masonry had been thrown high into the air to rain down on the church and some can still be seen to this day, left as a monument in Church Walk, with a plaque telling the dreadful tale.

THESE STONES
WITH BURNING TIMBER
AND RED HOT IRON BARS,
WERE BLOWN ONTO THE
ROOF, AND INTO THE
CHURCH, BY THE
EXPLOSION IN MILLGATE
OCT 6TH 1854.
WEIGHT OF THE LARGEST
STONE 481/2 CWT.

The plaque and monument in Church Walk

Worse still, not only had St Mary's been bombarded by the violence of the explosion, but red-hot fragments, burning materials and huge stones were thrown clear across the river, to rain down on the densely packed crowds who had gathered on Newcastle Quay to watch the blaze.

Eye-witnesses on the Gateshead side of the river testified that "the crowd upon the Quayside and Sandhill were mown down as though by a discharge of artillery, many being rendered insensible from the shock, others temporarily suffocated by the vapour, and many more wounded by the flying debris".

It is said that, initially, an awful silence succeeded the blast, but the dread calm was broken within a few seconds as the victims who had been stunned regained consciousness, at which time a terrible wail arose, although many were "far removed from all earthly sufferings, their voices never to be heard again".

As the *Shields Gazette* reported, "in a moment the shops of Messrs Spencer & Sons, Messrs Smith & Ormston and Messrs Smith & Co. were ablaze, whilst uninjured bystanders rushed off in all directions in search of safety".

The Infirmary, Forth Banks, built in 1752
It served the citizens of Newcastle well until the beginning of the
twentieth century, when it was demolished and replaced by the R.V.I

Many bodies of the dead and dying, struck by the falling debris, however, were left behind, strewn across the quayside in heaps. Even the ships in the river were ablaze, their crews desperately trying to control the flames, some leaping overboard into the oily swirling waters, now illuminated with bright reflections like the fires of hell. All of the shop fronts on the Quayside, the Sandhill and the Side were blown out and the gas lights of the town for a square mile around the disaster were extinguished, further adding to the danger and confusion of the scene. People staggered about screaming in the dark, and many a bleeding apparition appeared from narrow side streets, where shattered windows had showered deadly shards of glass down on to the hapless crowds. All of the available fire engines being in Gateshead, the fire spread rapidly through the ancient warren of buildings on and above Newcastle Quay. Soon the public houses of Mr Teasdale (*The Dun Cow*) and Mr Batey (*The Golden Anchor*) were consumed and the flames leapt up George Stairs to destroy the houses packed at the head of that ancient thoroughfare.

Now people were attempting to rescue the wounded, carrying them on doors and shutters to the infirmary, where they were tended and, in some cases, dreadful operations were carried out. Ann Laidler, a poor spinster, expired after both of her crushed legs had been cut off. The most common injuries were head wounds, however, many with fractured skulls, and they survived "in a more or less addled condition" after their heads had been bound up.

Fifty-eight people were so seriously injured as to be immediately admitted to the hospital, where fifteen died. The facilities being swamped by the demand, however, no fewer than sixty-three other persons, whose injuries would normally have qualified them for immediate admittance, were turned away after they had received rudimentary treatment as "out-patients".

But on the Gateshead side of the river, matters were even worse. Hillgate, the street in which the conflagration had begun, had been crowded with incautious onlookers at the time of the explosion. In addition to these gawpers, some leading citizens of the town were on hand, lending the weight of their presence and experience to direct the firefighters. Among these were magistrates and town councillors, besides influential gentlemen and businessmen, all attempting to do their civic duty by co-ordinating the efforts to contain the flames. The buildings of Hillgate were several stories high and the thoroughfare extremely narrow.

A similar street to Hillgate, lined with warehouses.
But this street, in Newcastle, is about twice as wide.

Into this narrow canyon the burning rubbish was hurled with great force by the blast. Literally hundreds of tons of burning debris rained down upon the defenceless heads of that unfortunate throng. Within an instant, firefighters, onlookers and all were buried to a depth of several feet by the burning remnants of the collapsed buildings. Though the loss of life was never accurately recorded, there was no hope of survival for those who had been in the immediate vicinity of the blast. Many perished so entirely as to leave no trace when the rubble was cleared.

Furthermore, many of the fire engines themselves were buried in Hillgate so that those firemen and soldiers who remained uninjured were hampered in their efforts to contain the advance of the flames.

No engine at all was available on the Newcastle side of the river until the engine of the North-Eastern Railway Company turned up on the scene and rendered invaluable assistance. Meanwhile, the floating engine of South Shields was on its way up the Tyne, the blast having been heard at the mouth of the river and the volunteer firemen having turned out their engine immediately, without waiting to enquire as to the cause or extent of the disaster. Engines were also on their way from Sunderland and by rail from as far afield as Durham where, even at that great distance, the blast had been clearly heard.

But meanwhile the fire had free rein through the ancient half-timbered warren of buildings on the Quay, making its way both northwards up Grinding Chare, racing through the old warehouses towards Butcher's Bank, and eastwards along the range of old buildings facing out on to the Quay itself. The shops of Mr Atkin, bookseller, Mr Turnbull, watchmaker, and the *Grey Horse Inn* succumbed to the blaze.

Fire had even broken out in the "High Town", a huge beam of burning timber having been propelled by the original blast fully half a mile, where it had fallen through the roof of a workshop belonging to Mr J Edgar at the back of Pilgrim Street. In Pilgrim Street itself, another huge beam, over ten feet long and eight inches square, weighing more than three hundredweight, was thrown through the roof of *The Ridley Arms Inn*, three-quarters of a mile from the scene of the explosion. A new conflagration immediately took hold and, despite the desperate efforts of neighbours, soon consumed many adjoining tenements, workshops and the grocer's shop of Mrs Ann Shield. As the sun rose on the carnage, it began to look as though the whole of the ancient heart of the town would be consumed by the dreadful blaze.

In fact the blaze was not brought under control until the engines from neighbouring towns, together with their willing volunteers, arrived on the scene, and it was a full day later before the City of Newcastle could officially be declared safe from a general conflagration.

At that time the bodies of those who had perished were at last rescued from the charred ruins on both sides of the river. Amongst the bodies recognised were those of the unfortunate Ensign Paynter and Corporal Stephenson, one of those under his command. Also in a fit condition for identification were the remains of Mr Pattinson and Mr Hamilton, businessmen of the town, and Mr Duke, a bricklayer, along with his entire family. Nearby, a charred and crumbling mass, bearing no resemblance to humanity, was presumed to be the body of Mr Alex Dobson, son of the famous architect, by reason that it was wearing a piece of his coat and his bunch of keys. Other fragments of bodies which bore marks of identification were those of Mr Davidson (a signet ring), Mr Thomas Sharp, gentleman, (a gold watch) and one of the volunteer firemen, who still clutched a molten piece of firehose nozzle in his charred hands. But many other corpses and remnants remained unidentifiable, being shockingly mangled and burned. No trace of the body of Mr Bertram, the unfortunate owner of the premises in which the explosion occurred, was ever found.

Hornsby's Chare, one of the ancient wynds destroyed by the Fire

And now that the fire had been brought under control, an immediate outcry arose to ascertain the cause of the catastrophe and bring those responsible to book. Rumours were spreading that gunpowder, illegally and secretly stored in Bertram's warehouse, had been the cause of the dreadful explosion which had caused such terrible damage and loss of life. The very morning that the bodies of the victims were recovered from the rubble, an inquest was convened at Gateshead Town Hall.

The Inquest

The inquest was opened at 10.00 am on Saturday the 7th October 1854 at Gateshead Town Hall by the coroner of Chester Ward, Mr J.M Flavell, who swore in the following jury;

John Greene (foreman), Bryan J Prockter, Matthew Thompson, Samuel Neville, John Vickers, Henry L Monro, John Sowerby, John Golightly, Joseph Abbot Hymers, Robert Coulthard, Joseph Fenwick and Edward Bruce.

Also present were many leading citizens of the town, including the Mayor, the Town Clerk and Mr Liddell, the local M.P. After the opening remarks of the coroner, the foreman of the jury, Mr Greene, asked leave to immediately state that there was no foundation whatsoever to the foolish and, indeed, malicious rumours which were circulating that the cause of the explosion had been gunpowder illegally stored on the premises.

The coroner drily remarked that that was the very purpose of the enquiry and that the issue of the cause of the fire, *and the explosion*, would be investigated in due course, at which time he wished to hear "*every* person who could give evidence on the subject". Then, despite the foreman of the jury's evident anxiety to exclude such speculation, one of the very first witnesses called, Sergeant Robert Sloan, of the 26th Regiment, gave evidence that the explosion in the warehouse was *very* like that of gunpowder. In answer to a query from a juror as to his expertise in such matters, he replied that he had seen action in the storming of the forts at Shanghai, China, and well knew the sight, sound and smell of a gunpowder explosion. But no, he had *not* smelled gunpowder after the explosion, as the smell of sulphur had excluded all else.

This led the coroner to call upon the warehouseman of the place which exploded, Mr Percival Smith, to give a list of articles stored within the warehouse at the time of the fire. The list given included many tons of sulphur, in various consignments, and, among other less significant items, much nitrate of soda. However, there was no charcoal (an essential ingredient of gunpowder) present, he added, a statement which was later proven to be untrue, and certainly he could testify that no gunpowder had been stored on the premises at any time.

Doubt was cast upon the accuracy of his statement, however, when the total quantities given were compared to the subtotals, floor by floor, which he gave for each of the seven stories of the building. Quite simply, the totals did not add up, the total for sulphur, for instance, being almost 1000 tons out! Difficulties arose in giving accurate totals because the floors of the building were not regular, he said, sometimes running one into the other, so that there was a possibility of double-counting the quantities on each separate flat. The unfortunate impression given was one of hopeless confusion and it appeared that he was at a loss to give an accurate account of the contents of the warehouse which had been under his charge.

Percival Smith, Warehouseman,
but no mathematician!

But now, when asked to state the name of his employer, the first sensation of the inquest emerged. He was employed by the agent Mr Sissons, who acted on behalf of the County Fire Office! Mr Bertram having mortgaged his premises to that Institution, they had foreclosed on him some time previously. It appeared that the very Institution charged with protecting the citizens of the townships from fire *owned* the offending warehouse and, consequently, that august body was itself liable for any misdemeanors which had resulted from its misuse! Mr Sissons was immediately called to the witness box.

Mr Sissons, after confirming that he acted as agent for the Fire Office, raised the point that, the premises being a "free warehouse", the goods stored there did not belong to his masters, but to the persons who had paid a fee to store them there. Insofar as they declared the nature of the items they deposited in the warehouse, the owners were bound to accept them as such. The implication here was not lost on the coroner or other members of the court. Was it possible then that gunpowder had been smuggled into the warehouse under a false title, or even brought there surreptitiously by night without the owners' knowledge?

As to the first suggestion, Mr Sissons did not think it at all possible. He declared that, though the premises had a river frontage, and the owners of goods had their own keys for the parts of the premises they rented, he himself had the sole outer key. To test the validity of the second suggestion, a juryman then asked a question concerning a consignment of eight tons of arsenic, which had been delivered to the warehouse in June. This consignment, which belonged to Messrs Coll Taylor & Co, was stored in iron-hooped barrels of the same type commonly used for gunpowder.

.

Could gunpowder not have been smuggled into the premises in this guise? Mr George Blair, the waterman who delivered this consignment was called to testify and positively refuted such a claim. He had handled gunpowder before, he stated, and knew it to weigh less than half that of a similar quantity of arsenic. He had taken the arsenic on board his lighter from the ship *Helston* and offloaded it himself at the warehouse quayside. He would have immediately noticed had any of the barrels been light.

But during the discussion of the handling of past consignments of gunpowder on Newcastle and Gateshead Quays, an interesting fact came to light. It emerged that the foreman of the jury, Mr Greene, owned a magazine at Elswick from which he, quite legally, sold gunpowder "in small quantities" to those who required it. He was quick to deny, however, that Messrs Coll Taylor had ever been customers. In fact, there was no evidence whatsoever that the aforementioned had ever bought gunpowder from any source at any time.

Leaving the vexed question of the presence of gunpowder, the coroner then enquired whether any of the other goods stored on the premises were explosive, either in themselves or taken together in combination? Expert witness was required on this point and the coroner ordered that a qualified chemist be appointed to advise the court.

The name of Mr Hugh Lee Pattinson, of Stots House, near Boldon, was put forward and, though some objections were raised as to his impartiality because his own company, the Gateshead Fell Alkali Works, used the premises in question for storage from time to time, the coroner approved his appointment and asked that he be requested to attend when next the inquest resumed.

Tyneside worthies discuss the case.

Adjourning the proceedings until the following Wednesday, Mr Flavell further ordered Mr Sissons, agent for the warehouse, to prepare an *accurate* written statement of the quantities of goods which had been stored in it at the time of the explosion and *their position relative to one another*.

Day excursionists inspect the burned-out ruins

Excitement reached fever pitch on both sides of the Tyne during the four days which passed until the adjourned inquest resumed. The North-Eastern Railway was even obliged to put on extra excursion trains for the crowds who flocked in from the surrounding countryside to gawp at the blackened ruins and to speculate on their cause. To add to the excitement, there were rumours of interference with witnesses, of threats to those who meant to come forward and testify that gunpowder *had* been the cause of the explosion..

But, if gunpowder *had* been stored on the premises, who had put it there and for what purpose? Some muttered darkly that the authorities knew more than was being admitted.

Mr Palmerston himself, the Prime Minister, was taking an interest and had sent a representative north, a certain Captain Du Cane, who meant to attend the inquest and observe its proceedings. This was a mystery indeed - what cause had the central government to want to keep such a close eye on what was after all, no matter how great the catastrophe, a purely local matter?

Mr Palmerston, Prime Minister.

At 10.00am on Wednesday the 11th October, the inquest resumed, Captain Du Cane being introduced and taking his seat alongside the coroner as he presided over the court. Outside, a noisy throng had been locked out and the public galleries were full to bursting point.

The day's proceedings began with an immediate sensation when Mr Schorey, the Superintendant of the Gateshead Police, rose to bring to the court's attention several letters he had received during the recess. These alluded to "certain parties and their alleged dealings with gunpowder", one of the parties named being the foreman of the jury, Mr Greene. That worthy, though strenuously denying all such claims of involvement, offered his resignation from the jury at once. Accepting his offer, the coroner remarked that though he would not have requested it, he "thought it better that he should retire" and a new foreman, Mr. John Sowerby, was immediately appointed.

And now a succession of witnesses were called who, it was alleged, had previously stated that they had heard that gunpowder had been stored on the premises. One by one, these witnesses repudiated their statements, denying that they had ever said or believed such a thing. These witnesses included a Newcastle magistrate, Mr Robert Plummer. He had *not* said that he believed gunpowder had been stored in the warehouse, he said, he had merely been repeating a rumour, utterly without foundation, which he had heard. Another who now denied ever having said that he knew of gunpowder being stored at the scene of the explosion was Mr Alexander George Gray. He knew nothing of gunpowder being stored at Hillgate but admitted that he had remonstrated with his onetime employers, Messrs Clarke and Dunn, about the excessive quantities they had used to keep at their premises at Walker.

When asked what had become of this gunpowder, Gray said he did not know, but some of it had subsequently been removed. He did not know if it had been taken to Bertram's Warehouse *because he went by Hillgate less frequently now.*

Mr Charles Dunn, of the firm Clarke and Dunn, Wharfemongers, was now called and testified that his company did indeed, quite legally and safely, store gunpowder at Walker, at a premises owned by The Corporation and under the strict supervision of a person named Davison. A juryman immediately challenged him to say how much gunpowder was stored at this location, but the coroner intervened. It was not the business of the inquest to enquire into the commercial affairs of witnesses, he said, and excused the witness from answering the question.

The coroner now called upon the expert witness, Mr Pattinson, to give evidence as to the explosive potential of the contents of the warehouse, a more accurate and comprehensive list of which had now been furnished by Mr Sissons.

It was now admitted that there had been a quanitity of charcoal present, and thus all the ingredients of gunpowder *had* been stored in the warehouse, though not together and not in a volatile mixture. Furthermore, Mr Pattinson expressed the opinion that no single product stored in the warehouse was potentially explosive in itself, nor indeed were any two of the products, nor even any three of them when mixed together in "rough quantities", but thought that the sudden introduction of water into such a mixture could give rise to a violent reaction leading to an explosion. Indeed, he had tested his theory by practical experiment during the time that the inquest had been in recess, with positive results.

The coroner then agreed to adjourn the proceedings until Friday, the 13th October, to allow Mr Pattinson time to prepare a demonstration of his theory on the origin of the explosion for the benefit of the court.

It now appeared that, subject to Mr Pattinson being able to supply a sufficiently convincing demonstration of his theory, the cause of the explosion would be put down to chemical reaction, with no-one to blame, and the claims of gunpowder being surreptitiously stored on the premises would be dismissed.

This did not satisfy the poorer citizens of the riverside area, however, many of whom had lost everything, including friends and relatives, in the blast. They still earnestly believed that gunpowder had been the cause of the catastrophe, gunpowder illegally stored there by persons who must be brought to book and made to pay for their criminal act!

*The opening of the High Level Bridge by the Queen on the
6th October 1849, five years to a day before the Great Fire.
(from the Illustrated London News)*

During the two days of recess, far more important visitors came to Tyneside to inspect the ruins. The Royal Train, en route from Balmoral, stopped on the High Level Bridge, from which the Royal couple had a clear view of the devastated quays. A far less joyful scene met their eyes than when they had last visited the area to open the bridge. The Queen was much distressed and enquired after the welfare of the poor folk who had been made homeless, donating one hundred guineas to the relief fund. After a "melancholy" study of the wreckage, they went on their way.

The Royal visit had done little to dispel public outrage, however, so that, when the coroner re-opened the inquest, he found that new witnesses had now come forward who *were* perfectly willing to give evidence as to the presence of gunpowder at the warehouse on the night of the blast.

Mr John Atkinson, agent for Hawks' Ironworks, took the stand to testify that Robert Matthewson, a waterman, had informed him that George Marsh, another waterman, had told him that he (Marsh) had actually delivered gunpowder to Bertram's Warehouse in Hillgate. Another waterman, Bartholomew Cuthbertson, had substantiated this tale in his presence, declaring that he had stood in Fenwick's Entry, Newcastle Quay, directly opposite Bertram's Warehouse, and watched Marsh land the gunpowder in Hillgate.

Both watermen were called upon to testify and denied that they had told Mr. Atkinson any such thing, although Cuthbertson agreed that he had seen Marsh bringing a load of gunpowder up the river in his wherry a fortnight before the explosion, but he didn't know where he had landed it.

Mr Atkinson re-iterated his evidence, saying that both of these witnesses had made *written* statements addressed to Mr Schorey, the Police Superintendant, to the effect that Marsh had delivered the gunpowder to Bertram's. Where was that evidence now and why were they denying it? Mr Atkinson now further asserted that he knew another waterman, George Errington, who had told him that his wife had been present at Marsh's house when a man had come to caution him that he should say nothing about delivering gunpowder to Bertram's Warehouse. Who was this man and on whose behalf did he act?

More powerful evidence yet now emerged when a customs officer, Mr James Taylor, asserted that he had seen gunpowder taken out of Bertram's Warehouse. But when questioned as to when this had occurred, he admitted it had been over a year since, on the occasion of the Queen's birthday before last. The gunpowder had been used to fire a salute. Two 28lb kegs of it had been taken from a vault on the ground-floor on the right hand side of the cart entrance to the warehouse.

Mr Taylor could not say who had issued the powder, but George Richardson, a Royal Marine pensioner had carried it away in a wheelbarrow. To his certain knowledge, there were other occasions on which gunpowder had been taken from the same vault, occasions such as Waterloo Day and Ascension Day, when Richardson, because of his military training, had been required to fire a salute.

Richardson now took the stand and denied that he had ever gone to Bertram's Warehouse for gunpowder. The gunpowder was brought to him at Hawks' for the purpose of making the cartridges to fire the salute. He may have said to Taylor that the gunpowder came from Hillgate but, on second thoughts, he didn't know where it came from. He did not recall firing any salute on the occasion of the Queen's birthday before last.

In fact, he now thought that the last time he had fired such a salute had been in 1838, when he did indeed think that the powder came from Bertram's Warehouse in Hillgate. The warehouseman, Percival Smith, interposed to say that, since Bertram's Warehouse had not even been built until after 1838, his memory was indeed fallible!

Mr Richardson left the stand amidst laughter and it seemed that the case for gunpowder had received a mortal blow until the next witness gave his testimony. This was Thomas Hall, and he claimed that Peter Brown, a quayside labourer, had assisted two others to put nine tons of gunpowder into Bertram's Warehouse during the week before the explosion. Brown had told him as much, before two witnesses, on the morning of the explosion. Peter Brown having been killed in the explosion, he could not be called upon to repeat his claim, but the two witnesses to the conversation, Charles Hume, another quayside labourer, and Ralph Faddy, a waterman, were immediately called upon to corroborate this evidence.

Hume immediately confirmed that Brown had told him that he had loaded gunpowder into the Warehouse and, when questioned as to his reaction, told the court that;

"I called him a liar and offered to bet him five bob it wasn't true. He was then standing beside *The Grey Horse* public house on the Quay, looking at the fire. After telling me that, he went up the Quay towards Sandhill. He did not say where he was going, because he was frightened, but he told me;

"you will hear a bigger crack by and by, so I'll be going!"

Brown was standing here when he met Faddy

This last statement was met with sensation in the court and it was some time before the next witness, Ralph Faddy, could be heard. Faddy at once corroborated Hume's words and added that Brown had said to him;

"Man! What are you standing there for? You wouldn't be standing there if you knew what I know!"

When asked what Brown did next, Faddy said that he went away up the Quay and that his body had later been found in an entry, into which it had been blown by the force of the blast.

The court was then in such a state of excitement that the coroner thought it best to adjourn formal proceedings whilst the jury, himself and Mr Du Cane retired to the chemical works of Mr Pattinson, in Felling, where they were to witness certain experiments. The time then being 2 o'clock, the court was ordered to recess and reconvene at 10 o'clock on the following Wednesday. That would allow plenty time for Mr Pattinson's theories and experiments to be thoroughly considered. Possibly the coroner thought that the intervening five days would also allow time enough for public excitement over that day's proceedings to subside.

When the inquest resumed on the Wednesday following, the coroner began by saying he had received a reply from Lord Palmerston to the calls for a reward to be offered for proof that gunpowder had been stored at Bertram's Warehouse. It had been suggested that such an offer might counteract the threats of those who wished to suppress such evidence. The Noble Lord declined as "this would be a departure from established practice, and would be attended with inconvenience". As to the request that an impartial chemist be sent from further afield to attend the inquest, one would be appointed, but there would necessarily be delay and it was suggested that the inquest be further adjourned pending such an appointment.

Meanwhile, it was revealed that Mr Pattinson's experiments had indeed proven that the goods stored in the warehouse, when acted upon by sudden and copious quantities of water, were quite capable of exploding with a force sufficient to have caused the blast. The coroner and his jury were convinced on that point.

But the "gunpowder" lobby had not fired its last shot. Elizabeth Brown, the poor widow of Peter Brown, was ushered to the stand and testified that her deceased husband had often spoken to her of the gunpowder stored in Bertram's Warehouse. In fact, he had come home late one night a week before the explosion because he said that he had been loading powder into Bertram's.

"Did he say powder, or *gunpowder*" she was asked.

"He said powder, but I knew he meant gunpowder"

"Was it not true" she was asked "that her husband was a habitual drunkard, to such an extent that he often made himself ill with drink and often spoke nonsense?"

"Yes, he was a drunkard, but he never spoke to me of the gunpowder when he was drunk, he went straight to bed."

"Where was he when the fire broke out?"

"We were both abed" she replied "but he got up to witness the blaze, and told me that the whole of Gateshead would most certainly be blown up. He went off to the Quayside and his body was found in Grinding Chare".

Distraught, the widow was now led from the stand.

Peter Brown warns waterman Ralph Faddy that an explosion is about to occur

Mr Molteni, a cabinet-maker who had a shop in the lower part of Pilgrim Street, then testified that pieces of debris thrown through his roof by the explosion had been blackened *as though by gunpowder* and he had taken them to his insurance agent, Mr Henry Wilson, as proof. Mr Wilson confirmed this and said he had taken scrapings of black powder from the debris. These were now handed to the coroner for chemical analysis. Proceedings were then again adjourned to allow such analysis and further consideration of Mr Pattinson's experiments. The court was ordered to reconvene on Thursday 26th October, when it was also hoped that a government-appointed chemist might be a available to attend.

The government's chemist, Dr Taylor, Professor of Chemistry at King's College, London, was indeed present when the inquest reconvened. Both he and Mr Pattinson had analysed the powder scraped from the fragments and concluded that no trace of gunpowder could be found. Professor Taylor also put forward a theory of his own as to how the explosion could have "naturally" occurred. The rapid release of huge quantities of hot gas in such a confined space might well have generated enough energy to cause the warehouse to explode. In his opinion, and given the volatility of the chemicals stored, this was very likely to have caused the blast. Mr Pattinson, who stood by his "water" theory, respectfully demurred. Much technical debate between the two expert witnesses then ensued, so that there was little time for further witnesses to be called that day. In fact, no new witnesses came forward to support the "gunpowder" case during the following days of recess. The inquest had dragged on now for almost a month and, inevitably, in the absence of further sensations, public interest was beginning to wane. There is nothing new in politics, no matter what the "spin doctors" of the present day might think. Judicious adjournments, for increasing periods of time, had gradually damped down public interest until a "safe" verdict could be reached without outrage.

So it was that the jury was at last able to return an "open verdict" on the 2nd November and the coroner was finally able to close the inquest. The presence of gunpowder at Bertram's was never proven but the coroner expressed his belief that it had *not* been the cause of the explosion. Captain Du Cane, who had sat beside the coroner and advised him to the end, congratulated the jury on "the successful issue" to which they had brought the enquiry. Many questions remained unanswered, however, and there were many who remained unconvinced. The editor of the *Shields Gazette* certainly expressed the view of the majority when he concluded that "the real cause of the explosion is a mystery still".

Perhaps the shrewd mind of Prince Albert had provided a clue to the authorities' attitude when he had asked David Haggie, Gateshead's mayor;

"I suppose you will not rebuild the homes which have been destroyed?"

"I hope not" had replied His Worship the Mayor, "but I hope we shall be enabled to construct a splendid new quay."

The Royal observer had been silent awhile, then he had drily remarked;

"Well, there is never an evil but good comes of it."

"King Cholera" could no longer hold court on Newcastle and Gateshead Quays, but over eight hundred poor families were homeless and scores were dead.

They had paid a hard price.

Bibliography

The following books were used or consulted for both background and material;

The Making of the River Tyne, R.W Johnson, 1895
The Rhymes of the Northern Bards, Bell, 1812
The Northern Minstrel, Marshall 1806-7
The Newcastle Songster, Marshall, 1816
Sketches of the Coal Mines of Northumberland and Durham, T.H Hair
Victorian Britain (The North East), Frank Atkinson, 1989
Gatherings from the Pit Heaps, by "Coleman Collier", 1861
The Tyne and its Tributaries, W.J Palmer, 1882
Allan's Tyneside Songs, 1862 and 1895 editions
The Keelmen, Eric Forster, 1970
The River Tyne, James Guthrie, 1880

But most material was obtained from contemporary copies of the following newspapers and periodicals;

The Newcastle Weekly Chronicle, The Newcastle Courant, The Newcastle Advertiser, The North of England Advertiser, The Tyne Mercury, The Newcastle Garland, The North and South Shields Gazette, The Newcastle Evening Chronicle, Richardson's Table Book, The Monthly Chronicle, Punch Magazine, and The Illustrated London News